© 1992 Franklin Watts

Franklin Watts
96 Leonard Street
London
EC2A 4RH

Franklin Watts Australia
14 Mars Road
Lane Cove
NSW 2066

UK ISBN: 0 7496 0823 4

10 9 8 7 6 5 4 3 2 1

A CIP catalogue record for this book is available
from the British Library.

Editor: Sarah Ridley
Designer: Janet Watson
Illustrator: Linda Costello

Photographs: Eye Ubiquitous 9, 13, 14, 16(b),
19; Chris Fairclough Colour Library 10 (both);
Chris Fairclough/F Watts 20; Robert Harding
Picture Library cover, 7; courtesy of RoSPA 26;
ZEFA 22, 25.

Printed in Singapore

LIFT OFF!

LIGHT

Joy Richardson

FRANKLIN WATTS
London • New York • Sydney • Toronto

The biggest light of all

Most of our light comes from the sun.

The sun's light travels
millions of miles through space.
It is still very bright when we see it.

The atmosphere round the earth
makes the light scatter
right across the sky.

Clouds may hide the sun but
the light still shines through them.

Switching off the sun

The far-off sun lights up the earth during the day.

At night, our side of the earth turns away from the sun.

Darkness falls because the sun cannot shine through the earth. Light cannot curve round the sides. It can only travel in straight lines.

Making light

In the past, people only had
candles or lamps to light the dark.

Now we can also make
light by using electricity.

Electricity pushes through the
thin wire in a light bulb.
This makes the wire glow brightly.

In the daytime you hardly notice
the light from a light bulb.
At night it seems very powerful.

Invisible light

Light travels in lightwaves
which we cannot see.

The lightwaves spread
out in straight lines
until they reach something
blocking their path.

We can see people and buildings,
floors and furniture,
because light is falling on them.

We cannot see the lightwaves
travelling towards them.

A beam of light

If you shine a torch in the darkness,
the light spreads out in straight lines.
It fades as it travels further away.

If you shine it near your feet
it makes a small bright circle of light.

If you shine it on the ground further away
it makes a larger patch of weaker light.

As the light travels it may light up
mist, smoke or dust in the air.
This shows up the shape of the
spreading light beam.

Blocking the light

Clear glass is transparent.
Light passes straight through.

Clouds, water and patterned
glass are all translucent.
They let the light through
but blur the view.

Solid things, like walls and people,
do not let any light through.

They make shadows where
they block out the light.

Bending light

Light can be made to bend
in different directions.

Flat mirrors reflect the light
straight back into your eyes.

Mirror glass can be shaped
to bounce the light round a corner
to show what is coming.

The lenses in glasses are shaped
to bend the light slightly
on the way into your eyes,
to make things look clearer.

Light in your eyes

When you look at this book, some of the light which falls on it is reflected back into your eyes.

Lightwaves from the book pass through the little holes in your eyes called pupils.

They make an upside-down picture at the back of your eye.

Nerves take the light picture to your brain for sorting out.

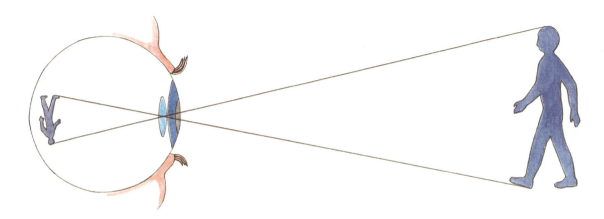

White light

Light contains all the
colours of the rainbow.
They mix together to make
pure white light.

We see a rainbow when the sun
shines through rain.
As light passes through
the raindrops, it splits up
into its separate colours.

Making colours

Whenever light falls on something, part of the light bounces off again.

We see this reflected light.

A red t-shirt only looks red because it soaks up all the other colours in the light. Only the red part of the light reflects off the t-shirt into our eyes.

Grass looks green because it reflects the green lightwaves but absorbs the other colours.

Light in the dark

Colours are brightest when
the light is strongest.
Colours disappear in the dark because
there is no light to be reflected.

Signposts and safety clothing
are made to show up in the dark.
When light falls on them
they reflect it brightly.

In complete darkness you would
not be able to see anything.
Nothing can be seen without light.

Light for life

Plants use light to make the food they need to grow.

Plants could not survive without light. Living creatures could not survive without plants.

Life depends on light.

Index

Atmosphere 6

Brain 21

Candles 11
Clouds 6, 17
Colours 23, 24, 27

Dark 11, 27
Darkness 8, 15, 27
Day 8
Daytime 11

Earth 6, 8
Electricity 11
Eyes 18, 21, 24

Glass 17, 18
Glasses 18

Lamps 11
Light 6, 8, 11, 12, 15, 17,
    18, 21, 23, 24, 27, 28
Light beam 15

Light bulb 11
Lightwaves 12, 21, 24

Mirrors 18

Nerves 21
Night 8, 11

Pupils 21

Rain 23
Rainbow 23

Shadows 17
Sky 6
Space 6
Sun 6, 8, 23

Torch 15
Translucent 17
Transparent 17

Water 17